Can you imagine what it would have been like to live on a farm long ago ??

You may think it would have been fun, but it was a lot of work for everyone!

Spinning thread and yarn to make cloth.

Weeding and caring for the "kitchen garden."

Churning butter

About 120 years ago, near the time of the Civil War, things began to change on farms to make work easier.

Cloth was *bought* at a store and sewn into clothes with a foot-powered machine.

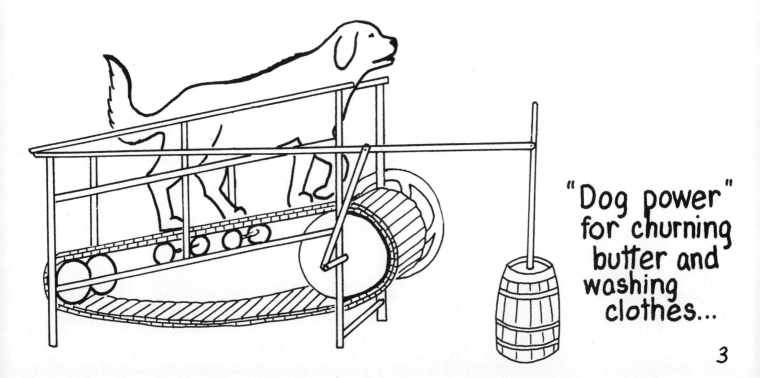

"Dog power" for churning butter and washing clothes...

Farmers were changing the kind of animals they used .

The old way was to use oxen to break through the tough prairie and woodland soil, which was full of rocks, roots, and stumps.

Oxen were very strong and easy to take care of, but they were very slow workers.

Farmers began using horses and machines to plow and plant.

6

Horses were harder to take care of, but they worked faster and could get more done.

After the wheat, oats, or rye were scattered by hand, the oxen pulled a harrow over the field to cover the seeds.

8 | Draw yourself leading the oxen on the left side.

Using horses and a "grain drill" machine helped to plant more seed faster.

After the oxen plowed the land in the Spring, planting was done by hand.

Draw yourself helping your father and brother plant corn. Plant it only where two plowed lines cross.

A faster way that was invented to plant the corn seeds was to use horses and a corn planter.

In the summer, fields were "cultivated" by hand to get rid of weeds between rows of corn or potatoes.

Farmers were always looking for new machines that were fast and that didn't hurt the corn plants when they cultivated.

Draw yourself on the horse leading the plow through the rows.

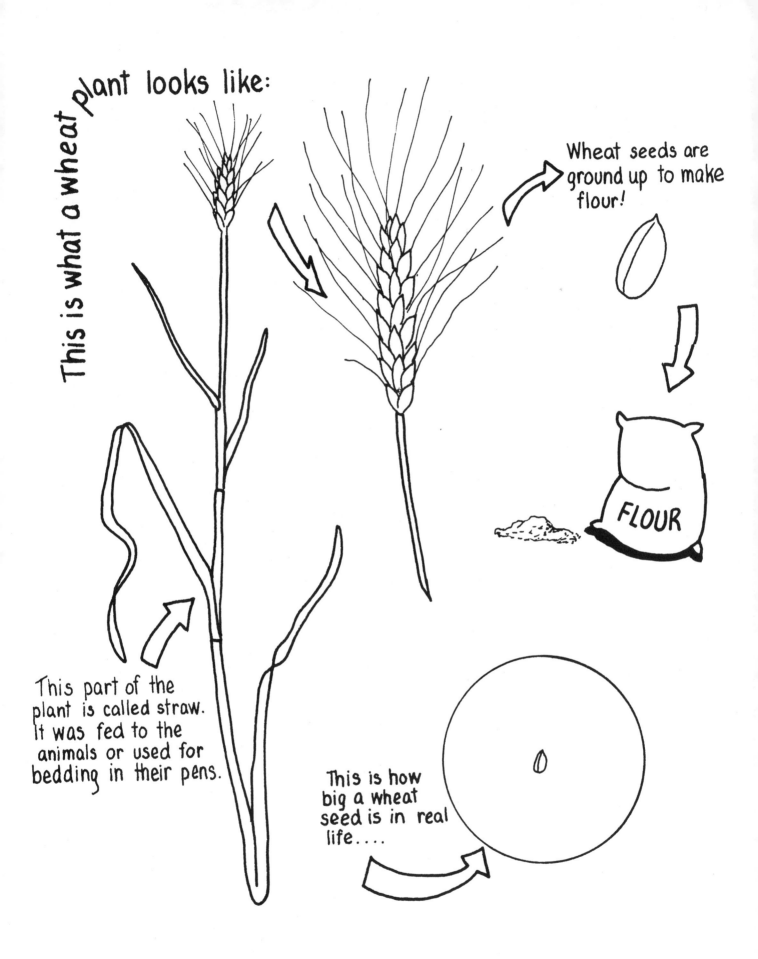

This is what a wheat plant looks like:

Wheat seeds are ground up to make flour!

FLOUR

This part of the plant is called straw. It was fed to the animals or used for bedding in their pens.

This is how big a wheat seed is in real life....

In Summer, hay and grain had to be gathered from the field for family and animal food.

This is the old, hard way to cut and gather wheat by hand.

The new machines did most of the work as they cut and raked wheat, oats, and rye into bundles. Men followed behind and tied up the bundles.

The farmer needed to separate the grain, or seeds, from the plant by *threshing* it.

In the old way, grain used to be separated by beating it with a "flail" in the fall or winter.

The threshing machine was invented and horses were soon providing the power.

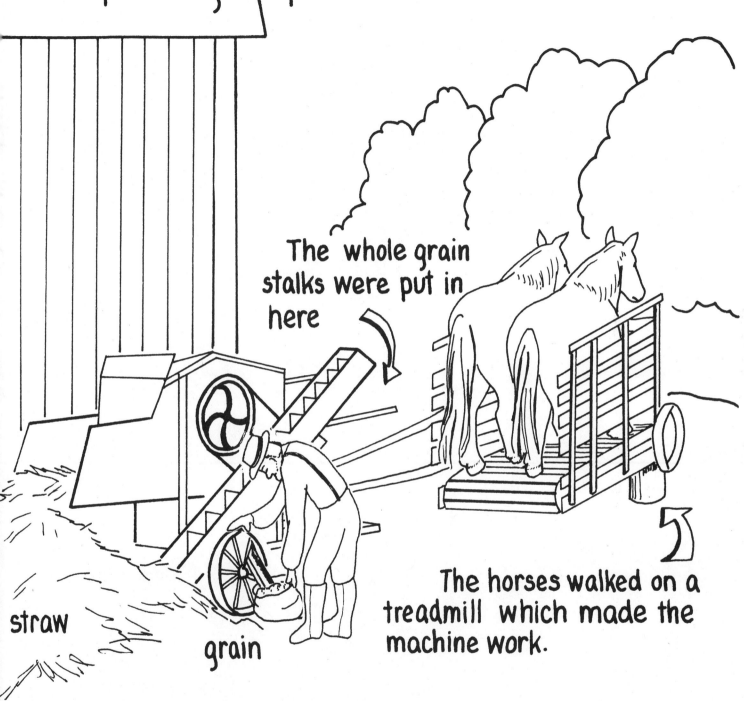

The whole grain stalks were put in here

straw

grain

The horses walked on a treadmill which made the machine work.

The threshing machine separated the crop into *straw* and *grain*.

After the hard work of harvest, the grain was taken to market to sell.

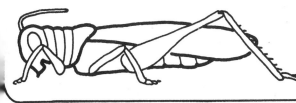

Life was hard. Sometimes the crops were eaten by grass-hoppers before harvest.

Sometimes people became sick, and many times doctors couldn't help them.

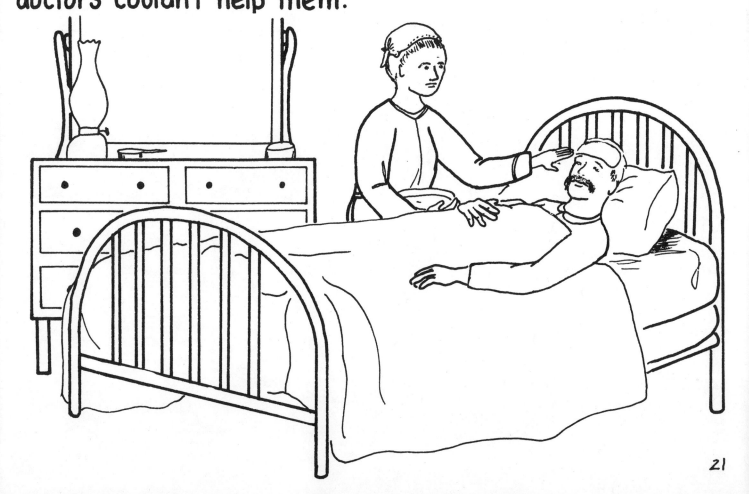

Before the changes, a family farm might look like this:

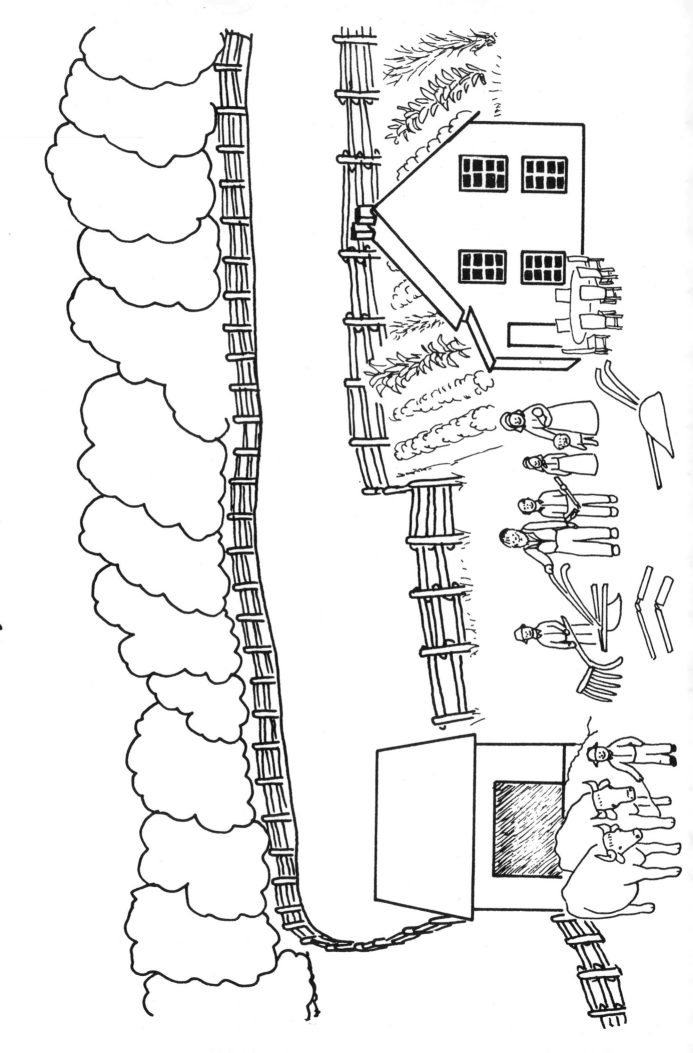

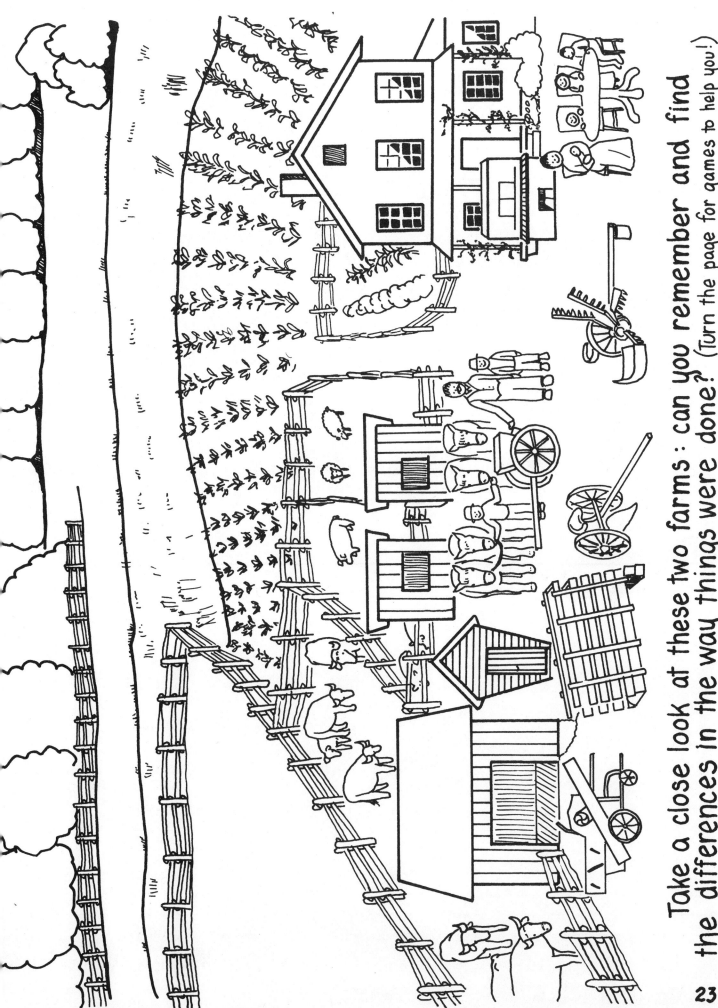

Take a close look at these two farms : can you remember and find the differences in the way things were done? (Turn the page for games to help you!)

Can you tell what each set of machines was used for? Also put a star next to the newer, faster machine.

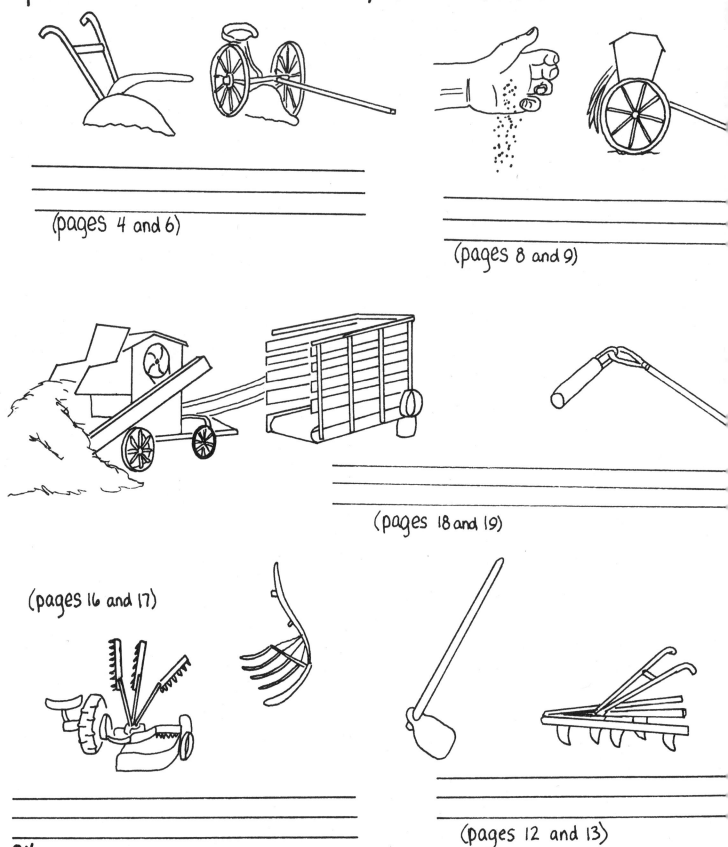

_____
_____
(pages 4 and 6)

_____
_____
(pages 8 and 9)

_____
_____
(pages 18 and 19)

(pages 16 and 17)

_____
_____

_____
(pages 12 and 13)

24 To see if your answers are correct, check the pages in this book that tell about each machine.

Everyone in the family had important, but different, jobs. They all worked together as a team, then relaxed with each other at night.

As the men's work got faster and easier, women's chores changed, too.

Instead of having to hoe in the fields,

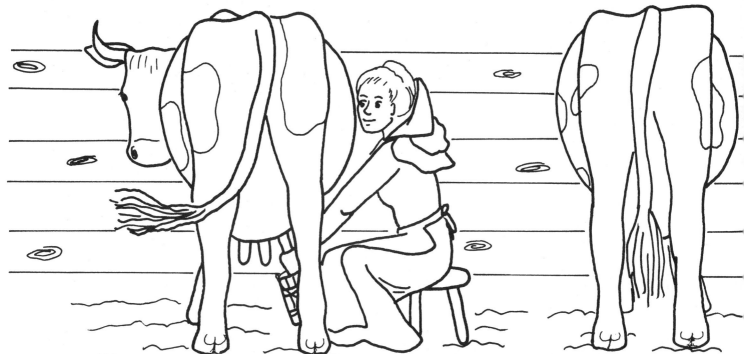

....they took care of more dairy cows and chickens...

... and often brought eggs and butter into town to sell.

The farm wife also took care of...

...the house...

...all of the cooking and baking...

...making, mending, and washing all the clothes and caring for small children.

Young boys stayed busy by...

...helping Father in the fields...

....feeding the animals....

chores chores chores chores chores chores chores chores chores chores chores chores chores chores chores chores chores chores chores

...gathering and cutting next winter's wood...

chores chores chores chores chores chores chores chores chores chores chores chores chores chores chores chores chores chores chores chores

28

....sweeping and cleaning....

chores chores chores chores chores chores chores chores

....helping in the kitchen....

chores chores chores chores chores chores chore

Girls' chores included....

feeding

chores chores chores chores chores chores chores chor

chicken

29

When the farm work was done, people visited neighbors, had picnics, and sometimes went to the fair.

What kinds of games did kids play way back then?

Ball and Cup

Use a small cup, a stick, some string and a small hard ball or acorn. Hold the stick and try to swing the ball into the cup. Whoever gets the most in the cup in 10 tries or 10 minutes is the winner!

What the Ship Comes Loaded With

All sit in a circle. A handkerchief tied into a ball is tossed around. The person catching it must quickly give the name of some object that begins with a certain letter that has been chosen. If the letter "C" was picked, they could say "Cakes," or "Cradle," or "Crickets" or "Clubs."

Threading the Needle

A boy and girl, each on a stool, make an arch that a circle of children pass through. Their hands drop over a person as the last line is sung.

The needle's eye
That doth supply
The thread that
runs so true;
Ah! Many a lass
Have I let pass
Because I
wanted you!!

As we go round the mulberry bush,
The mulberry bush, the mulberry bush,
As we go round the mulberry bush,
So early in the morning... ♪

This is the way we wash our clothes,
All of a Monday morning. ♪

This is the way we iron our clothes,
All of a Tuesday morning. ♪

This is the way we scrub our floor,
All of a Wednesday morning. ♪

This is the way we mend our clothes,
All of a Thursday morning. ♪

This is the way we sweep the house,
All of a Friday morning... ♪

This is the way we bake our bread,
All of a Saturday morning. ♪

This is the way we go to church,
All of a Sunday morning. ♪

Buzz Saw Toy...

is made with 2 small sticks, a large button, and 3 feet of string. To play, wind up by flipping the button around, then pulling the string in and out over and over. It will buzz loudly as it spins.